BEATING OCD AND ANXIETY

BEATING OCD AND ANXIETY

75 Tried and Tested Strategies for Sufferers and their
Supporters

Helena Tarrant

Cherish
EDITIONS

First published in Great Britain 2020 by Cherish Editions
Cherish Editions is a trading style of Shaw Callaghan Ltd & Shaw
Callaghan 23 USA, INC.
The Foundation Centre
Navigation House, 48 Millgate, Newark
Nottinghamshire NG24 4TS UK
www.triggerpublishing.com
Text Copyright © Helena Tarrant

British Library Cataloguing in Publication Data
A CIP catalogue record for this book is available upon request
from the British Library
ISBN: 9781913615093
This book is also available in eBook format:
ePUB: 9781913615109
Helena Tarrant has asserted her right under the Copyright, Design and
Patents Act 1988 to be identified as the author of this work
Illustrations by Helena Tarrant
Cover design by Bookollective
Typeset by Lapiz Digital Services

NOTE/DISCLAIMER

For Brian
whose loving support and practical help
have enabled me to write this book

ENDORSEMENTS

With a perfect blend of humility, insight and humour, Helena Tarrant dismantles fears, taboos and inhibitions around mental health and gives each of us encouragement on life's journey. Anyone who seeks a companion in a personal struggle or wishes to understand the mind of another will find disarming wisdom aplenty here.

— Samuel Wells, priest, writer and broadcaster

An expert by experience providing a view of helpful strategies for anxiety is very valuable.. Hopefully others will find this accessible and helpful.

— Dr Louise Waddington, clinical psychologist

This much-needed book, from one who has lived with anxiety and OCD, is invaluable both for those struggling with these conditions, and for those needing to understand what a sufferer is going through. Very readable and delightfully illustrated, with a touch of humour, this book is the guide many have been seeking.

— Rela Iwano, counsellor and psychotherapist

INTRODUCTION

This book started as an as aide-memoire for myself. I was
diagnosed with Obsessive Compulsive Disorder (OCD) in
my twenties and Generalized Anxiety Disorder (GAD) some
years later, although I have been over-anxious for as long as I
remember.

This is a set of anxiety-management strategies that work for
me. Most of them are based on Cognitive Behavioural Therapy
(CBT). Some are strategies that I have learnt formally through
therapy. Others have been developed from strategies that began in
therapy and that I then developed to be most effective for my own
anxiety disorder.

I hope that sharing these strategies will help others who
suffer from anxiety, whether diagnosed or not, and also those
who support them; supporting someone with anxiety disorders
demands a lot of patience and understanding.

I also hope you enjoy my cartoons! They are intended to
illustrate my points and highlight the humorous side of a very
distressing set of problems.

DIY ANXIETY TOOLKIT

My hope is for this book to provide a toolkit of practical insights, ideas and strategies so that you have a collection of techniques you can draw from to manage your anxiety at any time.

There are over 75 very practical strategies and tips in this book. They are highlighted to help you find them quickly. I have also repeated them at the end of each chapter. I have used all of them at different times. I see them as my Life Toolkit, and they have really helped me to cope effectively with, and largely overcome, my Obsessive Compulsive Disorder (OCD) and Generalized Anxiety Disorder (GAD).

The idea of the Toolkit is to provide you with an accessible and readily useable set of strategies that will allow you to thrive in daily life. You can tailor your toolkit to your own anxieties and needs as you go along, and access it whenever you need it.

None of the strategies involve keeping extensive records, exercising, setting aside a block of time each day or setting aside a physical space. Whilst these approaches can be of value, I found they were not practicable for me.

Instead, the strategies can all be practised during a normal busy day.

CONTENTS

CONTENTS

CHAPTER 1

THE NATURE AND CAUSES OF ANXIETY

What is Anxiety?

Anxiety takes several different forms, and many sufferers have more than one type. In this book I focus on the two forms that primarily affect me – Obsessive Compulsive Disorder (OCD) and Generalized Anxiety Disorder (GAD).

Here are these two disorders in a nutshell, according to online NHS definitions.

OBSESSIVE COMPULSIVE DISORDER (OCD)
"If you have OCD, you'll usually experience frequent obsessive thoughts and compulsive behaviours.
- an obsession is an unwanted and unpleasant thought, image or urge that repeatedly enters your mind, causing feelings of anxiety, disgust or unease
- a compulsion is a repetitive behaviour or mental act that you feel you need to carry out to try to temporarily relieve the unpleasant feelings brought on by the obsessive thought"

GENERALIZED ANXIETY DISORDER (GAD)
"GAD is a long-term condition that causes you to feel anxious about a wide range of situations and issues, rather than one specific event.

People with GAD feel anxious most days and often struggle to remember the last time they felt relaxed.

As soon as one anxious thought is resolved, another may appear about a different issue."

OCD has entered popular language to mean someone who is fastidious or a bit obsessive about certain things.

But sufferers of *real* OCD and other anxiety disorders can feel highly distressed and *imprisoned* by them, spending hours of their lives performing rituals and seeking reassurance, only for their anxiety and obsessive compulsive behaviours to get worse.

Thankfully, awareness of conditions such as OCD and GAD has been growing in recent years in line with rising mental health awareness, and this is a good thing.

You're Not Alone

Although anxiety can make you feel very lonely, you are not alone, as the following data from the NHS regarding both OCD and GAD demonstrates:

"What we know about OCD is that the condition affects as many as 12 in every 1,000 people (1.2% of the population) – from young children to adults, regardless of gender, social or cultural background."

"GAD is estimated to affect up to 5% of the UK population." (50 out of every thousand people)

Because many people are probably suffering in silence, the number of people with OCD, GAD, or both, is likely to be higher in reality.

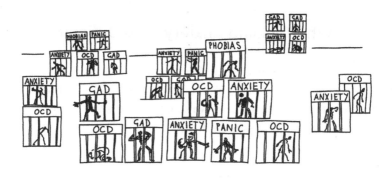

The Spider's Web

ANXIETY
SPIDER

Recently I was watching a fly caught in a spider's web. Although the web looked delicate, and the fly was large, the harder the fly worked to try to free itself from the web, the more it trapped itself in.

Living with OCD or GAD is like being this fly caught in the spider's web in that the more energy you expend *fighting* the fear and anxiety, the more it traps you and the less strength you have, even though the worries that plague you can seem very insubstantial and unlikely to others.

Why Tackling Anxiety is so Difficult

One of the most distressing and exasperating things about anxiety conditions is that a rational and common-sense approach has very limited effectiveness. No sooner is one worry settled than another tends to present itself.

Like a leaky pipe, if I stop one leak, water will just start springing out elsewhere. Trying to fix the individual worries only makes the problem worse. OCD and GAD worries need to be tackled by managing the underlying anxiety, rather than tackling the individual worries that present themselves. The individual worries are only the outward manifestations of the root cause.

I once worked as a clinic administrator. We had a call from a patient requesting a referral to a thoracic surgeon. A day or two later, the same patient rang again asking for a gastroenterologist. A couple of days later they wanted a neurologist, and so on.

After several of these calls, the GP referred the patient to a psychiatrist, because it was clear that the patient's problem was one of anxiety.

The patient did not recognize this themselves, and was prepared to go through endless sets of worrying appointments and a huge amount of money (the clinic was private), seeking reassurance for one individual worry after another.

If I have an anxious thought, such as, "My partner is late and is not answering his phone. Has something happened?", a natural thing to do is reassure myself and go through the logical reasons why he might be late.

However, while doing this will calm the worry in *most* people, it can have the opposite effect in GAD-afflicted people.

For these people, thinking on the worry can magnify it, leading to mental gymnastics where, as one horrific image is counteracted, a worse one replaces it.

As well as resulting in negative thoughts and *worries*, anxiety can emerge in all sorts of odd *behaviours*.

For example, an old persistent worry of mine was whether I had locked the door properly when I left home to go out. Rather than checking the door once or twice, I might need to check it twenty times.

Like many anxiety-sufferers, I have also been prone to ritualizing behaviours, where I have needed to perform a certain action repeatedly, such a touching a particular item a certain number of times; I go into more detail about these types of behaviours in Chapter Three: Anxiety Behaviours (i).

Because OCD and GAD worries generally cannot be counteracted with logic, reassurance often fuels the fire and makes the problems worse, not better. I explore this in Chapter Nine: The Need to Seek Reassurance.

'Help' from loved ones, therefore, can sadly make things worse sometimes, and can be desperately frustrating for the person trying to help.

The good news, however, is that there are ways in which family and friends can give crucial support, once the principles of useful support are understood (see Chapter Fourteen: It's Not All About Me).

Why Do I Get So Anxious?

The specific causes of OCD and GAD are not yet known.

But one theory is that our innate healthy fear to ensure survival – the 'fight or flight' response – remains as it was millions of years ago, and anxiety sufferers have difficulty controlling it. We therefore retain an exaggerated form of fear that we do not need in modern life.

Although the causes are not known, it has been established that OCD and GAD are not 'modern' conditions; research has shown that they have been present in many different populations through the years.

I have a couple of my own thoughts regarding the causes of my anxiety:

I believe there is a link between anxiety and lack of confidence. They feed off each other. I explore this concept in Chapter Sixteen: Alpha and Delta Behaviours.

I also believe there is a link between anxiety and creativity in that, if imagination and creativity are suppressed, they will find an outlet in endless fabrications and imagined scenarios. I have therefore found it very helpful to 'vent' or release my creativity in order to reduce the imagined scenarios that emerge from my anxiety. This is something I return to in Chapter Thirteen: Intolerance of Uncertainty.

CHAPTER 2

STARTING WITH THE BASICS

Focusing on the Management of Anxiety, Not Its Causes

Research is ongoing as to the causes of anxiety conditions.

Asking myself why I get so anxious can be useful to a point. But pondering at length on the reasons behind my anxiety is generally not helpful.

The important thing is to learn how to manage anxiety, rather than speculate as to its causes.

The good news is that, although there is, as yet, no known cure, anxiety can be managed very effectively, and quite quickly, using a range of strategies, such as the ones in this book.

As it is difficult to live with someone with anxiety, anxiety management techniques can also mean the difference between relationships lasting and not lasting.

It's best not to ponder too much about *why* I'm in an anxious state. I must just concentrate on finding a way out of it.

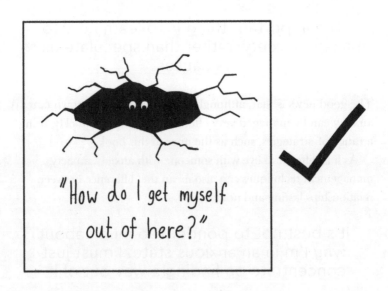

Applying anxiety management strategies will make life feel fulfilling and enjoyable rather than miserable and distressing.

THE ANXIETY CYCLE

Anxiety traps the mind in a cycle.

Anxious thoughts lead to negative emotions, such as fear and feeling desperate. These lead to compensatory behaviours, such as over-checking, seeking reassurance and ritualization. And these then reinforce the anxious thoughts.

Physical symptoms, such as shallow breathing, sweating, heart palpitations and a feeling of blood draining, can also occur in varying degrees.

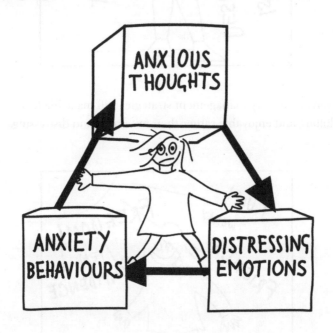

BREAKING THE ANXIETY CYCLE

It does not help to have someone tell you, "You shouldn't worry. Worry won't change anything".

I have known all my life that I am over-anxious, and that worrying doesn't affect outcomes. As such, suggestions that I have no need to worry are extremely frustrating, however well meant.

Instead, I must break the Anxiety Cycle to stop the continual fuelling of anxiety and free myself. So how do I go about breaking this cycle?

It is almost impossible to control thoughts and emotions. However, it *is* possible (albeit difficult) to change *behaviours*.

The Anxiety Cycle must therefore be tackled at the *behaviour* level.

This is the basis of Cognitive Behavioural Therapy (CBT) – the clue's in the name!

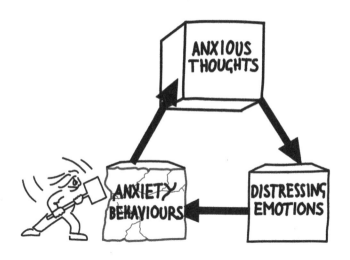

No therapist would say that the aim of CBT is to change someone's personality. Rather, it helps to manage anxiety so that the personality can manifest itself. Until medical science comes up with an easier way to manage anxiety, patients need to manage it themselves with the support of therapists, friends and family.

Life Toolkit strategies from this chapter:

1. The important thing is to learn how to manage anxiety, rather than speculate as to its causes.
2. It's best not to ponder too much on *why* you're in an anxious state, just concentrate on finding a way out of it.
3. The Anxiety Cycle must be tackled at the *behaviour* level.

CHAPTER 3

ANXIETY BEHAVIOURS (I): OUTWARD AND HIDDEN BEHAVIOURS, RITUALIZING, SUPERSTITIONS AND REPETITIVE CHECKING

Recognizing Anxiety Behaviours

What are anxiety behaviours? And how can I recognize them so that I can start tackling them?

Anxiety behaviours are the things I do to mitigate the uncomfortable feelings that I experience when I am anxious.

Anxiety behaviours vary from person to person. Examples are repeatedly checking things (locks, lights and so on) and excessive hand-washing. It is, of course, important for everyone to do things like washing hands and checking locks for health and safety purposes. But if I am doing them *excessively* – well beyond what is necessary – and especially if I am becoming distressed by not being able to 'get away' from these actions, my behaviour is being driven by anxiety rather than need.

Anxiety behaviours might also include rituals – for instance walking on the lines in the pavement, or doing things in a certain order or a certain number of times – with a conviction that this will in some way safeguard myself and others.

Outward Anxiety Behaviours

Outward anxiety behaviours are easy to recognize. They are visible – physical actions that other people can see.

To know if a behaviour is anxiety-related, I ask myself whether the behaviour would look odd if I saw *another* person doing it.

Repeatedly washing hands for several minutes, for example (assuming that this is in an everyday context rather than somewhere like an operating theatre), would generally be regarded as an odd behaviour.

Hidden Anxiety Behaviours

Hidden anxiety behaviours are those going on inside a person's head — so not seen by others from the outside, yet still happening.

They involve repeatedly doing something in the mind, such as visualizing a scenario or silently saying a certain phrase. Experts call such behaviours 'mental compulsions'.

When dealing with mental compulsions, the sufferer might be preoccupied and unable to engage properly in social situations.

It is more difficult to recognize *hidden* behaviours than *outward* behaviours, but, personally, I always find that, deep down, these mental compulsions don't feel quite normal.

I can check whether I have gone too far – in other words, slipped into anxiety behaviour – by asking myself, "Am I over-thinking this?" or by recognizing that I am mulling over unlikely or far-projected scenarios at length.

My partner or friends can really help by letting me bounce my concerns off them, too – so long as I'm not repeating them or going on at length!

Ritualizing

Many people ritualize to some degree, for instance, placing towels in the bathroom in a certain way. You do not have to suffer from GAD or OCD to be prone to mild forms of ritualizing.

However, a ritual, in an anxiety context, is a behaviour that someone feels absolutely compelled to perform and finds difficult to stop. Ritualizing is particularly prevalent in OCD.

It is a very easy anxiety behaviour to recognize as it tends to *look* odd. For me, it generally also *feels* odd, despite the compulsion driving the ritualizing.

The rituals are triggered by beliefs that something needs to be done in a certain way to prevent something bad from happening.

Before I learnt anxiety management strategies, I was very prone to ritualizing. My own ritualizing usually centred around touching things.

For example, I might think, "If I touch this post three times every time I go past it, people will be safe from terrorist attacks today" or, conversely, "If I *don't* put my hand on this wall, a loved one will die", and so on.

I remember being really distressed at the age of about seven because I had trodden on a piece of grass on the pavement and then had a strong compulsion that I needed to tread on it an even (rather than odd) number of times.

When I didn't get to tread on it a second time to make the number even, I was plagued with a horrible feeling, like an itch but much more distressing, that I must find this piece of grass and tread on it again. I didn't understand why I had this feeling but it was there.

Rituals versus Superstitions

Anxiety-based rituals are like superstitions in that they cannot be tackled with reason or rational thought. Indeed, attempting to do this can often just strengthen the need to perform the ritual.

Superstitious beliefs are held by a lot of people at some level. Many of us believe, for example, that a groom must not see his bride's wedding dress before the wedding, or that someone who breaks a mirror might have seven years' bad luck. Conversely, a black cat crossing your path means good luck.

Actors believe that saying 'Macbeth' before a performance will cause a disaster, so they might refer to "the Scottish Play" instead. And if "Macbeth" *is* said, a ritual must be performed to remove the curse brought about by having uttered the word.

Many commonly held superstitious beliefs are probably derived from traditions that started for a logical reason. For example, it's a superstition that you shouldn't walk under a ladder.

From a practical perspective, this makes sense: someone on the ladder may drop something on you. However, even if the practical reason seldom now applies, it is remarkable just how strongly we stick to these superstitious beliefs. Clearly superstition is a normal activity of the human psyche – up to a point.

Rituals could be viewed as a form of personal superstition, and many people experience both ritualizing and superstition in a mild form.

Learning to Control Ritualizing

Although it is really hard for OCD sufferers to keep their ritualizing to a level that most people would consider 'normal', ritualizing behaviours *can* be managed with gradual reduction. I explain this in the example below.

Courage and determination are needed for this, but the results are worth it.

Some years ago I felt compelled to touch a certain gatepost three times on my way to work each day. In therapy, this ritual became a focus for managing my ritualizing behaviour. My doctor suggested that I try to touch the post only twice the next day.

When I reduced the number of times I touched the gatepost from three to two, I felt very uncomfortable, and experienced a sense of panic. I was very tempted to turn back after taking a few steps and touch the post one more time, to make it up to three times.

However, as I walked on further, and the distance between me and the post increased, the feelings of discomfort and panic started to subside.

The following day, I managed to touch the post just twice again, rather than three times. And after another few days, I could touch it once only.

A couple of weeks after I started the reduction process,
I managed not to touch the post at all.

The gradual reduction of ritualizing is not always smooth.
Occasionally I would touch the post three times again after
managing just twice for a few days, or I would touch it twice
again after managing just once for a few days.

My doctor made it very clear that I should not be disappointed
or angry with myself if this happened. Reducing an OCD or
GAD behaviour is extremely difficult, so there were bound to be
times when the reduction would not go as smoothly as I wished.

The key message from my doctor was not to feel downcast, and
to keep persisting. A 'slip' was nearly always short-lived – for just a
day or two – rather than a 'back to square one' scenario.

It is important, when training oneself to
manage anxiety, not to be discouraged by
any lapses.

I am still prone to ritualizing from time to time. However, I used to ritualize about 50-100 times a day. Nowadays, months go by without my ritualizing at all.

Some of my anxiety behaviours reassert themselves in stressful times or situations. I have therefore sometimes had to repeat the reduction process. However, I can now do this on my own without the help of therapy, and it always takes only a fraction of the time that it did at first.

This proves that, with persistence, behaviour management can and does work. Not *all* of my anxiety behaviours have disappeared completely but most of them have, and those that remain have been so significantly minimized that they no longer make my life difficult. The feelings of desperation that used to go with them are now non-existent.

So, although anxiety has no known cure at present, persistence with anxiety management can significantly lessen its impact. The fact that I don't ritualize any more is one example of this.

Seeing the Funny Side

A sense of humour can be enormously helpful in managing anxiety. For me, this has been particularly true for ritualizing behaviour.

One day I was walking from the bus stop after school with a friend. We were both about 14. At this time one of my OCD behaviours was to have to touch things an even number of times.

I brushed against a car that was parked outside one of the houses, and immediately put my hand on it to ensure I had touched it twice. The friend, knowing about my OCD (although neither of us knew at the time what OCD was), thought she would have some fun with this and pushed me on to the car again, knowing I would have to touch it again, which I did.

For a couple of minutes my friend kept pushing me on to the car, and I kept putting my hand on it, until a woman came running out of the house towards us, shouting, "What are you doing to my car!?", as well she might.

At that point we both ran, and I didn't have time to worry about the number of times I was touching things!

Seeing the funny side of anxiety did not reduce anxiety behaviour in itself, but it could help me to let go of it more easily from time to time.

The Fear of Tempting Fate

A fear of tempting fate is another symptom of anxiety, although not one solely confined to people with anxiety conditions. This kind of fear might resonate with some people and mean nothing to others.

The fear is that the act of developing a strategy to cope with a potential bad thing makes the bad thing itself more likely to happen. An example would be a person not wanting to write a will because they think it will make their death more likely.

This fear of tempting fate can be very strong, so it doesn't help for others to dismiss it perfunctorily. It's important to know that it's OK to say, "I'm scared of this".

I have experienced a fear of tempting fate in writing this section: I feel worried that by *writing* about the fear of tempting fate, I could indeed be 'tempting fate' and that something bad will happen – work that one out!

Interestingly though, as I write about it, the fear is starting to lessen, which should come as no surprise to me, as I know, after a lifetime of training myself to handle irrational fears, that looking them in the face often means they become at least a little less strong.

Many types of anxious thoughts become less threatening if they are faced down, bit by bit. As with reducing ritualizing, it can be very hard, but persistence is worthwhile.

When I am afraid of tempting fate, I look the fear in the face and try to deal with it a little bit at a time.

Repetitive Checking

Constant checking is another classic OCD behaviour.

Many people have a tendency to double-check light switches or push their front door to check it is really shut, which is all good and normal.

OCD sufferers, however, are unable to stop at a normal level of checking. They are compelled to re-check the same thing repeatedly, as their checking goes into overdrive.

Like ritualizing, checking is a form of self-reassurance.

When I was prone to over-checking, a simple second's task, such as making sure that a light switch was off, or a door was locked, became a complicated, time-consuming and exasperating procedure. The checking made me run the risk of being late for work and other important appointments.

When I checked something, it was as if the action didn't 'log' in my head. I therefore couldn't be sure that I had checked, even though I knew, rationally, that I had. So I had to 'log' it again, yet again it wouldn't log – and so it continued.

There was often more than one thing to check, as there can be when leaving a house or office. Yet when I completed a round of checks, it was as if I hadn't started.

I was convinced that a disaster, such as a fire or a burglary, would result from my *not* checking.

As a result, I was unable to stop myself checking and re-checking light switches, doors, windows, devices and appliances every time I left the house or office. In one job, I checked everything in the office about 25 times before I left for the day.

This was one of the things that prompted me to seek professional therapeutic help for the first time.

I even sometimes turned off things that shouldn't have been turned off when I did my repetitive checks. For example, one morning I got in trouble with my boss because I had switched off the fax machine the night before, which prevented him seeing an important message that arrived from the US overnight.

As well as taking up a lot of time, there is often the added complication of sufferers trying to hide the ritualizing behaviour of over-checking at work or in social situations, which in itself can become tiring.

How to Stop Repetitive Checking

The good news is that checking behaviour can be controlled by gradually reducing it; I trained myself in this in the same way that I learnt to reduce my ritualizing.

Together, my doctor and I would work out a target that I thought might be realistic. For example, perhaps I could check the window latches just 18 times each, not 20 times, and tell him how I had got on at the next session.

Once I had achieved this, I could try reducing to 15 times, and start reducing the checking on something else – the light in the back office, for example.

One day I hit on the idea of making a list of all the things in the office that had to be checked. So, my focus moved to checking the list rather than the things themselves.

I put a tick beside each thing once I had checked it. The tick acted as external evidence that I didn't need to check again.

This did not stop the checking (I still over-checked!), but it was easier to check a list than to check all the things in themselves.

And this new reduction strategy was instrumental in speeding up the process of learning to reduce the checking further – and also in enabling me to eventually stop over-checking at the office altogether.

I was then able to use the same strategy in other situations. And, having been successful with the office checking, the strategy worked much more quickly when I applied it elsewhere. For example, at this time I also tended to over-check the locking of my car.

Whenever I left the car, I locked it, then checked it was locked by trying the door, then walked around and checked the other door, and checked the boot was locked, despite the fact that the car locked centrally.

I would walk around the car doing this about 15 times, and each time felt like the first round of checks.

Wonderfully, I was able to stop the car-checking quite quickly. Although it seemed to disappear by itself, it is much more likely that it happened as a by-product of the reduction training I was giving myself in other areas.

> Now, when I start to over-check things again, I am on the alert to deal with the checking immediately, and I start the same reduction strategy.

It only takes two or three brief reduction sessions now (of up to 30 seconds each) for me to see a difference. I have never needed to make a list again, although I still find it useful to keep this idea in mind for back-up.

At the time of writing this I still retain one or two checking procedures. For example, I still sometimes check the car by looking through the windows to check both doors once or twice after I have locked it.

I still have to listen to my 'mental alarm' about the car checking – if I catch myself checking the locking excessively, I must make the effort to stop.

Alarm bell - I know I'm starting to over-check

I mention this as a reminder that, although my anxiety can't be completely cured, anxiety behaviours *can* be got under control.

These days my anxiety is still strong enough for me to perform *slightly* odd behaviours, but not strong enough to be distressing or debilitating. And if I discovered that any of these behaviours were becoming distressing or annoying to someone else, I feel I would now be capable of stopping them permanently.

Car-checking is a visible, *outward* anxiety behaviour. I can use it as an example to test whether my behaviour is normal or slightly odd, as follows:

- Locking the car and trying the door briefly, or glancing back briefly, is *normal*.
- Locking the car, leaving, then going back to re-check, is *excessive*.
- Revisiting the car several times and/or peering into it at length, is *definitely excessive*.

If I have the feeling deep down that my behaviour is excessive, I use the gradual reduction strategies just discussed.

If ritualizing and checking behaviors are allowed to continue without being checked, it is very easy for them to become habits in themselves, which can then be much harder to stop.

Once I realized that I am prone to ritualizing and over-checking, I knew that it was important to nip the behaviour in the bud by stopping myself doing it as soon as I became aware of it.

I realized that some of my fears around failing to check things were stronger than others, depending on the focus, or 'trigger', of the fear.

For example, the fear of leaving the heating on was less strong for me than that of leaving the hairdryer on because, although leaving the heating on is expensive, it is not dangerous. It was therefore reasonably easy to prevent myself going back to check I had turned the heating off. However, the fear of leaving the hairdryer on was much harder to deal with and sometimes I did go back and check, despite knowing that the hairdryer would probably cut out automatically as a safety measure.

When I find myself indulging in a ritual that I realize I don't feel too bothered about (such as checking the heating in the above case), it's important that I stop doing it as soon as possible. Otherwise it's likely to get to a point where it is much harder to stop as it feels distressing.

When the urge to check something is less strong, I take the opportunity and *don't* check!

This will make me anxious *temporarily*, but the distress will gradually reduce, so it is a great opportunity to practise reduction behaviour.

Life Toolkit strategies from this chapter:

4. To know if a behaviour is anxiety-related, ask yourself whether the behaviour would look odd if you saw another person doing it.
5. You can check whether you have gone too far – in other words, slipped into anxiety behaviour – by asking yourself "Am I over-thinking this?" or by recognizing that you are mulling over unlikely or far-projected scenarios at length.
6. Although it is really hard for OCD sufferers to keep their ritualizing to a level that most people would consider 'normal', ritualizing behaviours *can* be managed with gradual *reduction*.
7. It is important, when training yourself to manage anxiety, not to be discouraged by any lapses.
8. Seeing the funny side of anxiety does not reduce anxiety behaviour in itself, but it can help you to let go of it more easily from time to time.
9. When you are afraid of tempting fate, look the fear in the face and try to deal with it a little bit at a time.
10. The good news is that checking behaviour can be controlled by gradually reducing it.
11. Focus on checking the list of things to check, rather than the things themselves.
12. When you start to over-check things again, be on the alert to deal with the checking immediately, and start the same reduction strategy.
13. When the urge to check something is less strong, take the opportunity and *don't* check!

CHAPTER 4

ANXIETY BEHAVIOURS (II): THE DISTORTION OF REALITY, DELUSIONS AND FALSE PERSPECTIVES

Living in a Self-Distorted World

Many of the anxiety behaviours going on inside our heads are not as straightforward as the mental compulsions described in Chapter Three, so can be more difficult to recognize. I would like to talk about these in the next few pages.

Living 'in my Head', Not in Reality

Mark Twain once said that his life was filled with "terrible misfortunes" – most of which he realized had never happened! Recently I was driving down a country road with which I was not familiar. It had a lot of hills and bends, and I was not used to this kind of driving, where the road is sometimes only visible for 30 to 40 metres ahead, or even less. I found I was unable to trust the road. Every time I could not see far ahead, which was most of the time, I would drop in speed and sometimes almost come to a standstill.

The reason for this was that I was imagining all sorts of deadly scenarios just ahead of me: "What if there is a broken-down vehicle in the middle of the road around the bend? What if there is a sudden turn just over the brow of this hill?" and so on.

Whereas other traffic was travelling comfortably at an even pace, my speed was erratic. I was driving 'in my head'; using 'what if' thinking, based on my imaginings.

Instead, I needed to focus my attention on what was actually *there*.

Difficult bends were highlighted with chevrons and heralded with warning signs. There was also signage for other potential hazards such as bridges, or narrowing roads, giving all drivers time to adjust speed, gear and so on.

I didn't *have* to imagine hazards because the information was provided in advance.

Dealing with the possibility of unpredictable things in the road, such as a break-down, was more difficult for me. So, here, I had to work on a balance of probabilities by recognizing that the likelihood of an accident being caused by a potential stationary vehicle suddenly blocking my path was *less* than the likelihood of an accident caused by my own currently erratic driving.

In fact, my erratic driving was likely to make *me* the cause of an unpredictable stoppage in the road, and turn my imaginary fear into a real danger for other drivers.

I needed to concentrate on the road – the signs, the other traffic and what was in front of me – rather than on my imagined worst-case scenarios.

Living with anxiety can feel like you're continually driving on a hazardous road like this. Rather than concentrating on what is real and right in front of you, half the mind is often occupied with unreal, imaginary calamities.

This makes life much more difficult and tiring than it needs to be. It can also be frustrating for family and friends of sufferers because it can seem to them that their loves ones are disconnected from them, in their preoccupation with imaginary events.

When I'm driving, I have learnt to focus on the actual road and the surroundings, rather than imagined scenarios just over the hill or around the next corner. . .
The fact that I have now learnt to do this when I drive reminds me that I must seek to *live* in this way too . . . and live in the real world around me, and not the imaginings in my head.

The Curse of Delusion

Another common anxiety behaviour is to submit to the delusion that catastrophic events are much more likely than the evidence indicates.

Given that we are all presented with a disproportionately negative view of life in the media these days, it can be all too easy to become deluded and feel that we are constantly surrounded by disaster.

We know, in theory, that this isn't true, and that disasters are simply treated as more newsworthy events than positive everyday happenings. But we can still be left buying into the delusion and feeling scared.

I recently read an article about a book entitled *The Power of Bad* (by John Tierney and Roy F Baumeister). The point is made in the book that more people actually die in *bathtubs* than in terrorist attacks. After all, while there are now many precautions in place to anticipate terrorist attacks, no one feels the need to ban bathtubs!

Similarly, we have all heard reassuring facts: for example, for every aircraft that crashes, millions fly safely.

I have often thought, "Yes I know all that, but that is no comfort to me. Just suppose I was one of the unlucky ones? The statistics would mean nothing. The fact that there is any chance at all makes this anxiety-worthy."

It would be wonderful if anxiety could be cured just by thinking *rationally* about the microscopic chances of disaster. But, unfortunately, as the anxious know, anxiety is more complicated than that.

It can, however, help to spend a moment from time to time at least *reminding* ourselves of the concept just described as 'disaster delusion'.

After all, most of us don't tend to think of taking a bath as a potentially fatal activity, so why obsessively worry about something like the chance of being killed in a terrorist attack when it is, apparently, three and a half-thousand times *less* likely than dying in the bathtub?

If I can remind myself of things like this, I can start to recognize the curse of delusion.

Unfortunately, one's whole perception of life can be severely coloured by delusions that unlikely disasters are more likely to happen than they actually are.

As a result, I used to live timidly in unconfident 'Delta' fashion (I talk more about this in Chapter Sixteen: Alpha and Delta Behaviours), and not make the most of life's many opportunities.

> It can be useful to use a visual mental prompt if you find yourself getting stuck in thoughts of disaster arising from imperceptibly small chances.

For example, you could bring to mind an image of the bath mentioned above as a reminder of the microscopic nature of negative events in general.

The Perspective-Distorting Lens of Anxiety

"Get it in perspective." You might, like me, have heard these words countless times, and got really fed up with them.

When someone delivers this 'advice', it sounds like a trite platitude; I have said it to myself plenty of times over the years when confronted with an individual worry, and it is usually ineffective.

Putting things in perspective is a tall order for everybody from time to time. For example, few people would be likely to feel entirely calm if stuck on a broken-down train travelling to a new job on their first day. At the time, this might feel like a complete disaster, as no-one is immune to feeling stressed or exasperated.

Anxiety distorts our sense of perspective very quickly. So, what can help us to keep things in better perspective?

Let us try a visual comparison.

Think of anxiety as being like a microscope.

If we look at a fly through a microscope, it looks enormous. We know the size of the fly in reality, but all we can see is a gigantic fly because the view in the microscope obliterates our view of everything else.

It follows from this then that, for example, something as simple as a cross word from a friend could, if viewed through a microscope lens, be viewed as something much more significant than it really is, such as the end of a friendship.

Seeing things in this 'microscope' way means we are likely to feel continually fearful and wrong-footed.

If, however, we can remind ourselves of the small size of the fly in reality, we can see that it is a miniscule thing that we don't need to be scared of.

When you sense that you have got a worry out of perspective, it can help to call on a visual prompt that represents the notion of perspective, such as the fly and microscope.

Although we know that many of the things we worry about are, like the fly, of tiny significance in the grand scheme of things, the distorting lens of anxiety tends to turn these things into mind-filling potential catastrophes.

Why does this happen when deep down we *know* the true scale of things? Why are we prone to looking into the microscope rather than looking around and about us?

Nobody really knows this as yet, because so far, a definite root cause of anxiety has not been found. However, an awareness of when we are starting to use microscopic vision, instead of taking a wider view, can be a good first stepping stone to starting to try to change the behaviour.

Life Toolkit strategies from this chapter:

14. Live in the real world around you, and not in the imaginings in your head.
15. It can be useful to use a visual mental prompt if you find yourself getting stuck in thoughts of disaster arising from imperceptibly small chances.
16. When you sense that you have got a worry out of perspective, it can help to call on a visual prompt that represents the notion of perspective, such as the fly and microscope.

CHAPTER 5

PRACTICAL AND HYPOTHETICAL WORRIES

Identifying Practical versus Hypothetical Worries

There are two main types of worry – known as **practical worries** and **hypothetical worries**.

Practical worries are those that everyone experiences as part of daily life. They are situations related to external things, such as the car breaking down, a troublesome tooth, demands for payments, and so on.

Hypothetical worries are those that exist only in our minds – things that have not happened but that we fear might happen. These sorts of worries often start with 'what if', such as...

- "What if I lose my job?"
- "What if my husband's plane crashes when he is travelling on business?"
- "What if that fish I just ate was undercooked?"

... and so on.

Hypothetical worries cannot be addressed in the same way as practical worries because they exist only in the mind with no self-evident solution.

There are different types of strategy for managing these different types of worry.

It is therefore important to know which type of worry you have at any given time so that you can implement the right type of strategy.

Being familiar with your preferred strategies and knowing you can implement them is key to managing anxiety.

If you are not sure whether your worry is practical or hypothetical, ask yourself the following question: "Can I do something practical about this worry right now?"

If the answer is yes, the worry is practical.

If the answer is no, the worry is hypothetical.

Sometimes, worries can be both practical and hypothetical. For example, a worry that starts as practical, such as, "I have a rash," can become a hypothetical one, such as, "What if the rash is a sign of something sinister?"

Dealing with Practical Worries

Practical worries can usually be directly addressed. By this I mean you can *do something about them!* For example, you can take a malfunctioning car to a garage, go to the dentist with a troublesome tooth, pay a parking ticket, send an email, run an errand, make a phone call or take whatever other immediate action is relevant to start alleviating the situation.

I dislike the hassle of dealing with practical worries because they take up time that I'd rather be spending on other things. I have to figure out the details of how to manage each specific problem that arises (such as deciding which garage to take the car to, or how to pay for the parking ticket). And I might even have to break some problems down into lots of more manageable bite-size chunks, perhaps asking for assistance from a friend or friends.

Although practical worries can therefore be stressful and bothersome, I know that once the worry has been dealt with, I can cease to worry, because the source of the worry will be gone.

As such, practical worries are not in themselves GAD-related, unless they bring about anxiety behaviours, or they start to meld into hypothetical worries.

Dealing with Hypothetical Worries

For people with an anxiety disorder, it is usually much harder to deal with hypothetical worries than practical ones.

This is because, by their nature, hypothetical worries are connected with imaginary scenarios that have not happened, and will most likely not happen at all. And because these worries are abstract, there are no self-evident solutions.

The intuitive thing for many is to try to dismiss a hypothetical worry by telling themselves they are being silly. This is often also the thing that friends will try to do. Sadly, as everyone afflicted with an anxiety disorder knows, this approach tends to have the opposite effect from what is intended in that the more you try to dismiss a hypothetical worry, the stronger it gets.

Soon it can become all-consuming, leaving you caught in a spider web of anxiety over something which, to outward appearances, might not even look like a worry at all – making it all the more distressing for the worrier and all the more confusing for the onlooker.

I explain below how I deal with hypothetical worries.

Worry Time and a Worry Diary

A very effective way that I learnt a couple of years ago of dealing with hypothetical worries is to use what are called **'Worry Time'** and a **'Worry Diary'**.

The principle of Worry Time is simple.

It is to set a particular 'Worry Time' in my day when I allow myself to worry. This way, when individual worries crop up, I can postpone them to this specific time later in the day.

The act of consciously postponing my worry helps to release its vice-grip on my mind in the short-term, allowing me to concentrate on what I am doing in the here and now.

I can tell any other worry that emerges during each day, "I will think about you at (say) five o'clock, so don't bother me until then, thanks."

Then when I reach the allotted time, I can turn my attention to my collection of worries.

It can be helpful to start a Worry Diary to note worries down as they occur during the day, so that I have a note of them for 'Worry Time'.

I find that externalizing the worries onto the page in this way helps to put them out of my head for the time being.

Alternatively, I can record my worries on my phone which is sometimes a more practicable, or less conspicuous, way to keep a 'diary'. There are also some good phone apps that have been specifically designed to help keep a Worry Diary.

When noting my worries, I started by noting down the worry, what time it occurred, the strength of the worry in terms of a percentage, and whether the worry was practical or hypothetical.

However, personally, after a few days of keeping a Worry Diary, I decided only to note hypothetical worries, as practical worries were less of a problem for me, and I didn't always note down the time or strength of each worry because I couldn't keep interrupting my work to record them in this detail.

The level of detail recorded is therefore a matter of personal preference. The main point is to externalize the worry by noting it down in preparation for Worry Time.

Once Worry Time is reached, it should not last more than about half an hour, and it can be much less than that, depending · on how much time is needed.

I have often found that worries felt much less distressing during Worry Time than when I had initially written them down. Often, one, more, or even all of them, had disappeared altogether.

I would highly recommend the Worry Diary and Worry Time strategies as being one of the most effective ways of managing anxiety.

These days I don't need a physical Worry Diary or structured Worry Time. Instead, I think in terms of a mental 'Worry Box'.

I mentally toss the worries in the Worry Box and come back to it later. However, I know that I can always go back to the full version of a Worry Diary and Worry Time if I need to.

Present Mind Focus

At the end of each 'Worry Time' session it is important to practise 'Present Mind Focus' – to bring me back to the here and now.

Present Mind Focus can also be practised at any other time if needed. For example, I use it from time to time to help me put intrusive hypothetical worries on to a mental 'shelf' when I am feeling mentally or even physically paralysed by anxiety.

Present Mind Focus has five components, although sometimes I only do one or two of the five if I'm short for time.

1. Mindfulness with the Senses
Use my senses to focus on the immediate surroundings:
- 5 things I can see
- 4 things I can hear
- 3 things I can feel
- 2 things I can smell
- 1 thing I can taste

2. Physical Mindfulness
I take 30 to 60 seconds to focus on my breathing and the positioning of my body.

If intrusive thoughts occur, I go back to the 'Mindfulness with the Senses' exercise.

3. Focus and Distraction
I spend a minute or two concentrating on a particular object nearby (such as a desk lamp), and describe it in writing or draw it.

4. Muscle Tense and Release
Starting with my hands, I clench them for Five seconds or so, then release, and concentrate on the pleasant feeling in the released muscles.

Then I progress to my arms, shoulders, feet, legs and torso, and finally I do the whole body together.

5. Diaphragmatic Breathing
I get comfortable, breathing in slowly and steadily through my nose to a count of five, and then out slowly and steadily through my mouth to a count of five. I concentrate on breathing deeply into my tummy, rather than into my chest.

I take as much time as I feel I need for these techniques. The times I have suggested are the ones that work for me personally, but everyone is different.

Life Toolkit strategies from this chapter:

17. It is important to know which type of worry you have at any given time so that you can implement the right type of strategy.
18. Set a particular 'Worry Time' in your day when you allow yourself to worry.
19. It can be helpful to start a Worry Diary to note worries down as they occur during the day, so that you have a note of them for 'Worry Time'.
20. With practice, you might not need a physical Worry Diary or structured Worry Time. Instead, you could think in terms of a mental 'Worry Box' to put your worry in.
21. At the end of each 'Worry Time' session it is important to practise 'Present Mind Focus'

CHAPTER 6

THE SOCIAL EFFECT OF ANXIETY

Alienation and Loneliness

Having an anxiety disorder is often desperately isolating.

Initially I found it impossible to describe the fear and desperation I experienced with GAD and OCD. Even if I managed to convey my feelings to another person, they would have difficulty in understanding why I got into such a state over such apparently small worries. They might be bemused and bewildered because there was seemingly nothing they could do or suggest that would relieve the discomfort of my anxiety.

Although everybody can get a bit over-anxious from time to time, there is no logical or common-sense reason that can explain the feelings associated with GAD and OCD. It is therefore difficult for people not affected by these conditions to understand them.

Confiding in a few people close to you can relieve a lot of the pressure of anxiety; friends can then help by reminding you of your coping strategies if you are experiencing difficulties.

How My Anxiety Behaviours Used to Affect Others

It is worth spending some time thinking about how other people are affected by one's anxiety behaviours.

Some of these effects are obvious. For example, suppose I am leaving my house with a partner or friend. They might understandably get impatient if I spend 15 minutes unnecessarily checking that I have locked the door.

At the same time, they want to help.

They might obligingly wait whilst I check I have locked the front door 20 times.

So, when I'm doing this, they might give reassurance after reassurance.

But unfortunately, my friends' obliging behaviour will not help, because they are actually allowing me to continue the anxiety behaviours.

Waiting whilst a door is checked is an obvious example of how an anxious person's behaviour can affect someone else. But some effects on others are more subtle.

For example, suppose I worry that travelling on the Underground is dangerous. If someone close to me is planning to use the Underground, I might want them to use different transport because I feel it would be safer. If I feel it is safer for them, I won't worry about them so much when they are on their journey.

The person who is travelling might not have my particular anxiety about the Underground. So if I inflict *my* anxiety on them by trying to encourage them to take a different route, I might cause them to have an anxiety about something that they didn't have before, *or* I might cause them to have a longer, more inconvenient, and perhaps more expensive journey.

In the meantime, there would be absolutely no guarantee that one form of travel would be safer for them than another.

Am I forcing someone else into a different course of action in order to mitigate a particular anxiety of my own?

Am I making up excuses as to why they should not travel on the Underground, when the real reason is to make things more comfortable for *me*?

Am I being honest with them about my anxiety, or am I giving them all sorts of 'fake' reasons to prevent them from going on the Underground, to disguise the real reason – that anxiety has taken a grip on me?

Be Honest With Others About Having Anxiety

Now I have learnt not to inflict my anxiety on others, but at first I wasn't aware how much I did this.

I've learnt it's best to be honest about my anxiety with those close to me.

This is for three very good reasons:

- Expecting others to put up with my anxiety behaviours without telling them about it may cause bemusement, irritation or exasperation, and put a strain on my relationship with that person, be it partner, family member, friend or colleague.

- Externalizing my anxiety by telling someone else about it immediately releases some of the pressure I experience when I am dealing with it alone.
- Other people can be instrumental in helping me manage my anxiety if I am honest with them.

Of course, I do not want to share the truth of my anxiety with everybody; indeed this would be unwise. But telling one or two trusted people, and explaining what I am doing to manage it, is likely to lead to their responding to that trust and being willing to support me.

I talk more about how friends and family can help to manage anxiety in Chapter Fourteen: It's Not All About Me. Support strategies can also be found interspersed elsewhere throughout the book.

Life Toolkit strategies from this chapter:

22. Confiding in a few people close to you can relieve a lot of the pressure of anxiety; friends can then help by reminding you of your coping strategies if you are experiencing difficulties.
23. It's best to be honest about your anxiety with those close to you.

CHAPTER 7

INTRUSIVE THOUGHTS

Recognizing Intrusive Thoughts

In CBT, 'intrusive thoughts' are unpleasant thoughts over which we feel we have no control and which can therefore make us feel mentally trapped.

A noted American author, Arthur Somers Roche, wrote, "Worry is a thin stream of fear trickling through the mind. If encouraged, it cuts a channel into which all other thoughts are drained."

Many intrusive thoughts take the form of hypothetical worries and quickly develop into a whole range of horrible case scenarios of disasters that I fear might happen.

Like a hypothetical worry, an intrusive thought cannot be overcome with common sense or logic. In fact, trying to do this can just strengthen its grip.

This point is excellently demonstrated in the following well-known exercise:

Try hard NOT to think about a spotted elephant for a couple of minutes.

So, what have you been thinking about for the last couple of minutes?

It is not distressing to have an intrusive thought about a spotted elephant, but it *is* distressing to have an intrusive thought about, say, an aeroplane crashing into the house.

If I try to counter the intrusive thought logically, it can get stronger and rapidly become all-consuming. Feelings of fear and panic can take over very quickly and lead to my being unable to concentrate on anything except the worrying thought.

I used to deliberately analyze intrusive thoughts, because I thought that if I could 'exorcise' the thought by examining it, it would neutralize it. But this really didn't work for me!

Intrusive GAD-related thoughts are often more difficult to handle than worries about real situations. For example, a close member of my family was once in danger in a foreign country. At the time that we heard this news, I was dealing with a worrying thought about whether I had contaminated somebody (see Chapter Nine for more about my irrational fear of this). Although I was desperately worried about the family member, the GAD-related worry about the contamination was the one that kept taking precedence in my head.

So, what strategies are there to bring intrusive thoughts back in proportion?

Managing Intrusive Thoughts

When an intrusive thought occurs, it can be useful to treat it like an annoying person who is sitting in my head and taunting me.

Because I know I can't get rid of it right now, I say to it "OK, sit there and do your worst. I've got to put up with you but I'm not going to give you any particular attention."

After a while, the thought tends to give up trying to annoy me, and its hold on me to start to fade.

If I concentrate on work, or get on with a simple task at home, the intrusive thought will usually fade more quickly. After half an hour or so, it might still be troubling me. But soon other thoughts start to take up space in my head and the intrusive thought shrinks or disappears altogether.

Another way of dealing with an intrusive thought is to think of it as an annoying *external* 'thing'.

When I find it bothering me, I put the 'thing' on a mental 'shelf' and be sure not to give it any undue attention. When I manage to do this, I am giving it a message that I'm not willing to let it dominate, so it fades more quickly.

An analogy for this is…

If I am drifting off to sleep and a noisy car alarm goes off, it is maddening. Why? Because it's loud and keeping me awake, of course. But it's also because I am powerless to stop it. However, dwelling on the noise and its effect on me, will only make me feel more bothered by it and less able to ignore it.

It's therefore best to accept that the noise is part of my general experience at the moment. This is not easy but if I can prevent the noise from being the overriding thing in my head, it will not have so much power over me, and therefore seem less bad, becoming more like inevitable background noise.

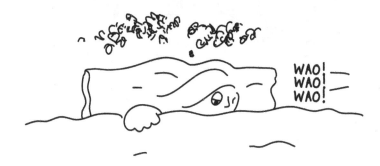

It used to take anything from about ten minutes to three days for one of my intrusive thoughts to fade completely. But by repeatedly using techniques such as the ones just described, they do not persist nowadays for more than about 40 minutes. And sometimes they disappear within less than two minutes.

Loosening the Paralysis of Intrusive Thoughts

Anxiety can be paralysing at times. Sometimes I have felt unable to do anything either mentally or physically. I have felt hopelessly burdened by the demon of a particular worry.

So it is good to have simple strategies to hand to help with this.

I have found when I've been incapacitated by anxiety that a physical response can work where other strategies have failed. And by this I don't mean exercise! – although it *is* recognized that exercise can indeed help anxiety-sufferers.

Instead, I mean actually physically changing my environment or activity, for example, by getting up from my desk or doing a practical task, such as the laundry.

The act of physically moving and concentrating on something simple will start to challenge the power of the anxious thought.

I have found that being forced to get on with the humdrum necessities of life has proven crucial in getting me through difficult times. Even the routine of getting up and going to work has often been a godsend.

Carrying out simple or mundane tasks might not make anxious thoughts disappear, but it always results in a loosening of the paralysis – getting the thoughts more into perspective so that they become more manageable.

It is not always helpful to try to 'get motivated' for a task to begin with. The key is to just start, with very simple bite-sized activities at first. And motivation sometimes follows.

Concentrating on work, or carrying out a simple task if at home, usually helps to get an intrusive thought into a more appropriate perspective.

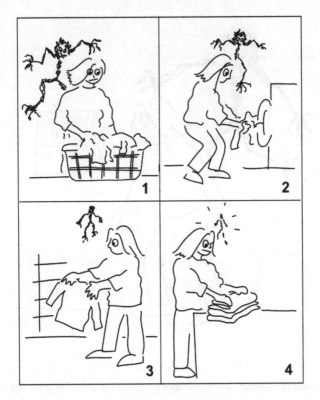

'Packaging' Intrusive Thoughts

It is both distressing and debilitating to be plagued by intrusive, worrying thoughts. Apart from making me upset and preoccupied, the thought can rattle around in my head, getting in the way, like something loose on the floor that I keep tripping over.

Packaging the worrying thought away in the manner I describe below might not make the worry *disappear*, but it will keep it out of my immediate mental environment so that I feel more in control.

- Imagine the worrying thought as a 'thing'.

- Put the thing into an imaginary box.

- Close the imaginary box.

- Put the box out of the way on a mental shelf.

- Now, whenever the worrying thought returns, don't think about the worry itself. Just imagine the box on the shelf.

This technique does not have to be used on its own. I sometimes find that a combination of, for example, this Worry Packaging exercise along with Worry Time (from Chapter Five) can be effective.

I use whichever techniques work for me, depending on the particular worry and what I find most effective. After a while I learnt what works best in different circumstances.

Recognizing Whether an Intrusive Thought is Normal

When I want to know if an intrusive thought is simply a 'normal' thought or one rooted in my anxiety, I use the following mental prompt:

- If I am hesitating or speculating about what to do in a worrying situation, the worry is most likely GAD or OCD-related.

- If I am not hesitating about responding to a worry, the worry is likely to be one that anyone else might have, to the same degree, in the same circumstances.

For example, if I saw a child about to cross the road in front of a car, I *wouldn't hesitate* to remove the child from danger. There is no doubt about it. This is clearly a 'normal' worry.

Knowing that an intrusive thought is GAD or OCD-related doesn't make it any easier to deal with, but it does make me feel that I have a bit more control over what is happening in my head.

Life Toolkit strategies from this chapter:

24. When an intrusive thought occurs, it can be useful to treat it like an annoying person who is sitting in your head and taunting you.
25. Another way of dealing with an intrusive thought is to think of it as an annoying *external* 'thing'.
26. Change your actual physical environment or activity, for example, by getting up from your desk or doing a practical task, such as the laundry.
27. It is not always helpful to try to 'get motivated' for a task to begin with. The key is to just start, with very simple bite-size activities at first. And motivation sometimes follows.
28. Concentrating on work, or carrying out a simple task if at home, usually helps to get an intrusive thought into a more appropriate perspective.
29. Packaging the worry away in the manner described below might not make the worry disappear, but it will keep it out of your immediate mental environment so that you feel more in control.
    - Imagine the worrying thought as a 'thing'.
    - Put the thing into an *imaginary* box.
    - Close your imaginary box.
    - Put the box out of the way on a mental shelf.
    - Whenever the worrying thought returns, don't think about the worry itself. Just imagine the box on the shelf.

CHAPTER 8

CATASTROPHIZING AND EXTRAPOLATING

What Do I Mean by Catastrophizing and Extrapolating?

Anxiety is fuelled largely by the mental processes I describe as catastrophizing and extrapolating. These are very rare for me now, but they used to happen many times in a day.

Catastrophizing is imagining the worst possible outcome in a scenario I am worrying about.

An example might be worrying about a loved one being a bit late home. Rather than keeping to the numerous realistic reasons as to why the person might have been held up, I tend to imagine immediately that something bad has happened to them, and see a terrible 'catastrophe' in my head, potentially in vivid and ghastly detail.

Extrapolating is the tendency to create a chain of events in one's mind, leading to a disastrous imagined conclusion. One tenuous link after another will be twisted into a highly unlikely but frightening set of imaginary circumstances with a terrible outcome.

Catastrophizing and extrapolating can get a firm grip in my mind very quickly, so it's worth looking at these behaviours more closely...

Catastrophizing

Much earlier in life, I went through a period of several months when I worried all the time that I might have serious illnesses.

I didn't have any symptoms, but if I detected anything that might possibly be a sign of something serious, I catastrophized. Fortunately this was before the Internet, otherwise I would probably have suffered even more by continually checking my symptoms there.

Obviously, any real signs of illness or things not seeming right in the body must be checked with a doctor.

However, the 'signs' that I was worried about rapidly shifted from one illness to another, and, if there was nothing to worry about, I started looking for other symptoms.

Although I didn't know it at the time, this was a sure sign that the worry was GAD-related and *not* real concern for my physical health.

My catastrophizing beliefs were similar to those of the clinic patient I described in Chapter One who kept ringing the doctor believing she had different things wrong with her.

Getting a Grip on Catastrophizing

Dealing with one worry and then going straight to another is generally a sign that I am catastrophizing and that there is no real substance to the worry. So I try to look at the catastrophizing objectively.

It is worth remembering that individual catastrophized worries will eventually go away because, as time passes, the imagined disaster hopefully does not occur.

But for catastrophized worries that stick around for longer, a trusted friend or family member may be able to help, such as by acknowledging my behaviours rather than dismissing them.

In the phase of my imaginary illnesses, my boyfriend at the time rang me one day and said, "How's it going? How's your cancer, and your Parkinson's Disease, and your heart problem?" He made me laugh at my own behaviour and thus look at it more objectively.

Getting a Grip on Extrapolating

If I am extrapolating and having difficulty letting go of a terrible imagined chain of events on my own, a friend or family member might be able to help here by pointing out when the extrapolation has gone too far.

This is something my partner helps me with by talking it through with me.

As with catastrophizing, a sense of humour applied to the situation can also work well.

Although my partner can point out that I am extrapolating, it is *me* who has to make a conscious effort to rein in the fear and prevent it from becoming a runaway horse. It won't happen by itself. However, reining in the fear gets easier the more I do it.

Reminder! Be Alert to Anxiety

Anxiety and intrusive thoughts can take hold very quickly, and the inevitable catastrophizing and extrapolation follow.

So I am always alert to intrusive thoughts starting to invade my mind.

When I am aware of 'anxiety alarm bells' ringing, I pay heed to the warning, and start my management strategy for the particular situation as soon as I can.

If I find myself starting to ritualize, for example, I don't let it drift, I start the reduction strategy straightaway.

Or if an intrusive thought starts to invade, I start the strategy for that as soon as I recognize it, and so on.

If a drift happens and I feel I haven't caught the anxiety soon enough, never mind. I just focus on the strategy again as soon as I am aware I have drifted.

Life Toolkit strategies from this chapter:

30. Dealing with one worry and then going straight to another is generally a sign that you are catastrophizing and that there is no real substance to the worry. So try to look at your catastrophizing objectively.

31. If you are extrapolating and having difficulty letting go of a terrible imagined chain of events on your own, a friend or family member might be able to help here by pointing out when the extrapolation has gone too far.

32. When you are aware of 'anxiety alarm bells' ringing, pay heed to the warning, and start your management strategy for the particular situation as soon as you can.

CHAPTER 9

THE NEED TO SEEK REASSURANCE

Is Reassurance Helpful?

Seeking reassurance is a very natural thing for a person to do when they are feeling worried.

In countless situations, this is the right thing to do. The reassurance will put the worry to rest and allow the worried person to move on.

For example, someone might worry about a medical symptom that has appeared recently. If their doctor tells them that the symptom is not a sign of anything serious, the person can be reassured and forget about it.

However, because hypothetical worries and intrusive thoughts normally cannot be countered with logical arguments, reassurance is often ineffective for people with GAD. Rather, it makes the worry worse, which leads to further reassurance seeking, which in turn leads to further anxiety, and so on.

In a very short time, the GAD-worrier can feel desperate.

I can best demonstrate this need for reassurance by explaining a fear I used to have that I was fatally contaminating other people. This fear would appear very frequently, albeit in different guises. And when plagued with it, I had an overwhelming need to seek reassurance that I was *not* contaminating people.

Seeking Reassurance: My True Story

My contamination fear centred around cup-washing.

At work, when it was my turn to wash up the coffee cups at the end of the day, I would wash them repeatedly.

I had an anxious thought that people would catch cancer from them, and that if I left even a tiny particle of contamination on one cup, I would be making someone ill.

So the washing, re-washing and repeated re-washing was a way of reassuring myself that the cups were not going to harm anybody.

If I was reassured by someone else, and told that the cups were fine, I was worried that they were wrong, and that if I followed their advice, I might still be responsible for contaminating others.

The washing behaviour became increasingly stressful because I was aware that it was odd and I knew that my colleagues were wondering what I was doing.

The more I washed the cups, the more desperate I felt as I knew that my fear of contamination would still be there after each round of washing. And I didn't know how I was going to stop the compulsion.

All the time, I knew that cancer is not contagious and that this particular anxiety was completely irrational.

The anxiety felt like climbing a mountain.

And the more I washed the cups, the taller the mountain grew, and the harder it was to stop washing the cups.

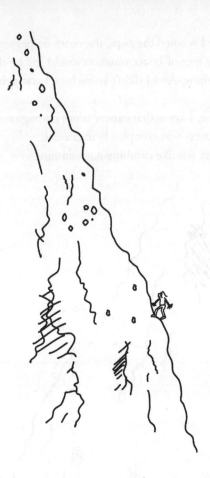

By continuing the washing, I was trying to continually reassure myself, which reinforced the grip of the anxiety and, in turn, led to the need for more reassurance and more washing. I was caught in a vicious anxiety–reassurance cycle.

Controlling the Need for Reassurance

I knew that the only way I could gain some control over the situation was to stop climbing (i.e. stop washing the cups) and take a different path to the one I felt compelled to follow.

And I knew that the only way to do this was to make myself unable to continue by physically removing myself from the cups and leaving the office.

When I did this, I experienced feelings of acute anxiety and appalling guilt – convinced that I was going to be responsible for making people ill.

As I walked to the station and boarded my train home, I felt acutely anxious that I was further removed from being able to wash the cups. I dreaded the results of my perceived scenario much more than I had ever dreaded any real-life situation.

By removing myself from the cups, I had decided to take the alternative path to the impossible one I was on. Yet on the journey home, I could think of nothing but the awful scene of a person, or people, becoming fatally ill because I had not washed the cups.

By the time I got home, however – about 45 minutes after leaving the office – I realized that, although I was still worried, I no longer felt quite as desperate.

As the evening wore on, my dreadful imaginary scenario became less convincing in my head.

And by the time I returned to the office the next morning and saw the cups in the cupboard, looking harmless, and everyone arriving for work as usual, I felt much less anxious, and my feelings of guilt had all but gone.

Rational thought was able to enter the space in my head that irrational fear had totally consumed the evening before.

I became aware that the path I was walking on *now* was a hugely easier one than the steep one I had been trapped on while washing the cups the day before.

Let us imagine for a moment that, rather than deciding to remove myself from the cup-washing situation, something external had stopped me from continuing on the washing path. For example, the caretaker might have come in and told me it was time to lock up, forcing me to leave.

If this had happened, the decision of leaving the cups would have been taken out of my hands, removing the fear and guilt I felt, and therefore my need for reassurance.

Similarly, if I had phoned someone to see if they thought the repeated cup-washing behaviour was odd and they had said, "Yes, of course it is. You don't need to do that," my fear and guilt would have started to dissolve because I could have told myself, "So-and-so said it was OK to stop, so it's *their* fault now if people get ill from the cups." Their words of advice, rather than the cup-washing itself, would have become the reassurance that I had been looking for.

Both these sets of circumstances would have made it easier for me to stop the cup-washing climb and take the alternative path, with much less fear and guilt.

However, being forced or persuaded to stop the cup washing by someone other than myself would have meant that I would have then been in exactly the same position – and back on the same steep path – the next time I had anxious thoughts around contamination.

The only way to take real control of the anxiety was to take the decision *myself* and steer myself on to the alternative path.

Once I had managed to do this, and to stay on this healthier path, the fear of giving people cancer started to break down.

This meant that when the anxiety of contamination on cups arose again, I was much better placed to stop myself washing the cups, and to take the alternative path. Although it was still very hard, I knew I could do it because I had done it before.

After a couple of months of repeating this strategy, the anxiety about cup contamination dissolved – and I was on the path to freedom!

And because I had conquered *this* fear, the path to freedom was also more attainable in other similar situations over the next few months, even though I did not conquer the anxious thoughts perfectly every time.

Because I trained myself over time to take the alternative path, I do not suffer nowadays from these sorts of irrational anxieties about putting people in danger. And I no longer need constant reassurance either from myself or others that everything will be OK.

When I still felt the need to keep asking for reassurance from others, I felt a horrible sense of dependency. I couldn't assert myself properly because I felt my opinions and self-sufficiency were undermined every time I had to go running back to one person or another to check something. I knew deep down that these things didn't really *need* checking, yet as soon as I received reassurance from the other person, I would feel alright about the thing in question.

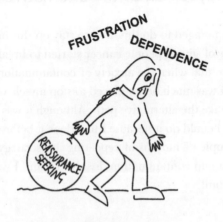

My life had been a constant run of dependency-based 'non-questions' such as, "Do you think this chicken is cooked properly?", "Did you see me turn the heater off?", "Do you think the receptionist got my appointment down properly?", "Do you think the delivery guy will realize I'm at the bottom of the road, not the top?", and so on.

I found nothing was as damaging to my sense of self-worth and self-esteem as this constant need to keep checking with other people that things were alright.

I therefore felt enormously liberated when I began to get my reassurance-seeking habits under control. It was as if a huge weight had been lifted off my shoulders, and my shackles had been removed.

I still get anxieties now and again for which I am tempted to seek reassurance. However, this is rare, as 99 times out of 100 I manage to control the need.

To do this,

I have to re-take the brave decision each time *not* to seek reassurance, and to stick with it. This used to be very tough to do, but I persisted, and it's much rarer and easier now – the strategy works!

And when anxieties of this 'catastrophe' type – whether about causing fire by leaving machines on or being responsible for other dangers – do emerge, I now have strategies to deal with them. And these strategies are vital.

Life Toolkit strategies from this chapter:

33. The only way to take real control of the anxiety is to take the decision *yourself* and steer *yourself* on to the alternative path.

34. Whenever you are aware that you are reassurance-seeking, take the brave decision *not* to seek reassurance every time you want to alleviate your anxiety, and stick to it.

CHAPTER 10

TIME-SENSITIVE WORRIES

What Do I Mean By Time-Sensitive Worries?

The most difficult anxieties for me in present life are the ones that I label 'time-sensitive'. By this I mean the ones that, by their nature, become more worrying as time goes on, and that, unlike most other types of worries I have looked at, *can* have a rational base.

Examples are waiting for a loved one to come home when they are late, or not being able to contact them when I am not sure where they are.

This type of worry is not confined to sufferers of anxiety disorders. Any parent, or person living with a loved one, is likely to be familiar with this type of worry.

The difference between an anxiety disorder point of view and a non-anxiety disorder point of view is that the anxious person will be likely to start worrying *before* it is necessary, or even when it is not necessary at all.

Dealing with Time-Sensitive Worries

Time-sensitive worries are more difficult to manage than other types of worry because, naturally, the longer I hear nothing from the person, the stronger the worry becomes.

However, I have worked out a step-by-step strategy for handling these Time-Sensitive worries, which I set out below.

The relevance of each point will depend on the person I am worrying about – their age, their normal habits, whether they have special needs, and so on.

Think of rational explanations

I think of a list of all the likely reasons why the person might be late or uncontactable. For example, their train might have been cancelled, they could have had a call from a friend and decided to make a detour to visit them, their phone might have run out of battery, they could be in a noisy place and unable hear their phone, etc.

Then, I make a positive effort not to repeatedly mull over these reasons, otherwise the worry will start amplifying itself in the same way as an intrusive thought does. I just mentally note the reasons and park them.

Defer the worry to a specific time

I use the Worry Time technique from Chapter Five to defer the worry to a later specific time if possible.

Or, if this feels impossible, I defer taking any action related to the worry to a later specific time. For example, I work out what I think would seem a reasonable period of time for the person to be delayed or out of reach, then I extend this by 20 minutes or half an hour, and tell myself that if I have not heard from the person after this extended period, then I am allowed to ring them.

Triangulate the worry

To triangulate something means to bring another perspective into a situation, so I share the worry with someone else. This helps me keep the worry in perspective and make the pressure feel less acute.

Now do something else

Until it is time to ring the person, I distract myself with
something that engages me but doesn't demand too much
mental effort – for example a craft project I'm involved in, or a
domestic task.

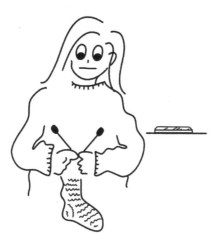

This is often much easier said than done, but the point is to make
the best positive effort I can.

Work out a joint strategy

If I ring the person after the time I have set myself, and I still
get no reply, then I talk with the person I have shared with, and
together we work out a reasonable time to leave until the next
attempt at contact.

I might at this point work some extra elements into my strategy.
For example, I might decide that if I don't get any reply at the
next contact attempt, I will check with a friend or colleague who I
know the person was seeing.

I remind myself that no news is good news, and that I would be
informed if there were any bad news.

If the Worry Turns Out to be a Real Concern

If I and my triangulating sharer still have not heard from the person within what we agreed was a generously reasonable length of time to hear from them, I am starting to move out of the realms of anxiety disorders into the same experience of worry that *anyone* would have in this situation.

I might then check in with a place where I know the person has been that day, check in with some of his friends and family, or I might even, eventually, contact the police. Hopefully I will have heard from the person well before then though.

Time-Sensitive Worries: More Mindset Tips

In a time-sensitive worry situation, it helps me to keep the following tips in mind in addition to working through my strategy:

Picture *a more likely* scenario.

When a disaster-case scenario concerning the person is running through my head, I make a conscious effort to overlay this with a mental picture of the person in a situation that is much more likely – such as enjoying themselves with friends and forgetting the time, or missing their train.

Look on the worry as an opportunity.

It is hellish to experience time-sensitive anxiety, but the experience can be turned to advantage by regarding it as practice for when this, or a similar worry, repeats itself in the future; that way, I will feel slightly less hellish the next time.

Use the hypothetical worry technique.

Apart from the strategy I am already practising, is there any more I can actually do about this worry right now?

Put the worry in context.

Why shouldn't the person be alright? Are they in a war zone or other dangerous environment?

Try not to indulge in catastrophizing.

I do my best to stop imagining a lot of awful case scenarios. It is easy for the mind to drift from one catastrophic scenario to another before I am even aware that I am worrying. Instead, I concentrate on a task I'm doing at the moment. Stoppage of catastrophizing does not happen on its own. Like all other anxiety management techniques, it takes a real, positive effort.

Get to the core of my unpleasant feeling.

What is really causing these unpleasant feelings? Am I actually worrying about the person's safety? Or am I experiencing something else, such as separation anxiety, or variation to a usual shared routine? Sometimes making an effort to really work out my feelings can help.

So, although time-sensitive worries can cause acute distress and be very debilitating, the good news is that the more this type of situation occurs, and the more familiar it becomes, the easier it will be to handle. Like other anxieties, when managed, I can eventually get the anxiety into perspective so that it is neither distressing nor disruptive.

Time-Sensitive Worries: Fear of Fear

When struggling with time-sensitive worries, I find that if I am not careful, I will quickly develop a worry *about* worry.

For example, a loved one might be out and about for several hours and will not be contactable until, say, 7 o'clock.

At about 4 o'clock I might start asking myself 'what if' questions, such as, "What if it gets to 7 o'clock and I haven't heard from them?" So, I can't even relax about it until 7 o'clock, because long before then I am anticipating the unpleasant worrying feelings that I *might* have at 7 o'clock.

Or perhaps I am due to fly abroad, and I fear that I will be worried about the security of my home when I am away. As a result, I might be worried that this fear will impinge on my enjoyment of the trip.

The first thing I do when I discover myself slipping into this kind of pattern of thinking is to remind myself that fear itself has never done me any harm (unless, of course, I were to be so preoccupied with fear that I stepped out in front of a moving car!).

Managing Fear of Fear

Fear is uncomfortable, but not in itself harmful.

So, if I start anticipating anxiety that might come at a later time, it is useful to resign myself to the fact that, when the time comes, I might just have to feel anxious. Too bad... I will just need to live with it for a while!

This resignation often results in my being able to let go of the 'fear of fear' at least a little bit, if not completely.

The technique is essentially the same as that I use for intrusive thoughts – to let the worry sit in my head but not to give it any special attention.

Despite having adopted and developed so many invaluable anxiety-management strategies over the years and knowing that there is plenty of professional help available, too, if needed, I still seem pretty determined to worry! The reason for this is a behaviour I call 'anxiety-fishing', which I talk about in Chapter Twelve: Anxiety-Fishing and Worry-Beliefs.

Life Toolkit strategies from this chapter:

35. Think of rational explanations for your worry, and make a positive effort not to repeatedly mull over them.
36. Defer the worry to a specific time, or at least defer any worry-related *action* to a specific time.
37. Triangulate the worry.
38. Now do something else.
39. Work out a joint strategy.
40. Picture *a more likely* scenario. When a disaster-case scenario concerning the person is running through your head, make a conscious effort to overlay this with a mental picture of the person in a situation that is much more likely
41. Look on the worry as an opportunity.
42. Use the hypothetical worry technique.
43. Put the worry in context.
44. Try not to indulge in catastrophizing.
45. Get to the core of your unpleasant feeling.
46. If you start anticipating anxiety that might come at a later time, it is useful to resign yourself to the fact that, when the time comes, you might just have to feel anxious for a while.

CHAPTER 11

GETTING TO THE NUB OF YOUR WORRY

A technique that works very well for me is to try to work out exactly where the root of a worry lies.

I talked about this in the previous chapter in relation to time-sensitive worries. It is also a good technique for GAD worries in general.

For example:

I'm worried about going away this weekend.

Why?

I'm worried about my cat when I'm away.

Why?

I will have to ask someone to feed my cat.

So?

I'm not sure if I will find someone free to feed my cat.

Ahh, so I'm actually worried about my cat and its feeding.

I have worked out in this instance that, as the cat owner, my general unease about going away is actually a specific practical worry that has an obvious solution – I need to find a friend who will feed my cat while I'm away, or put the cat in a cattery for that time.

Once I know exactly what I am worried about, and what kind of worry I have – practical or hypothetical, catastrophizing or extrapolation etc, I can choose and implement the right strategies to deal with the worry.

Getting to the nub of my surface worry has two additional benefits:

- I will almost certainly discover that my worry isn't as big as I first thought it was, and it will therefore feel less overwhelming and more manageable.
- I might discover that my feelings of discomfort are not due to anxiety at all, but due to something else. Perhaps I am worried about a loved one, but the cause of the distress is something other than worry, such as guilt because I feel I haven't spent enough time with them, a sense of failure that I haven't been persistent in helping them with something, or a sense of missing them.

Life Toolkit strategy from this chapter:

47. A technique that works very well for me is to try to work out exactly where the root of a worry lies.

CHAPTER 12

ANXIETY-FISHING AND WORRY-BELIEFS

Am I Anxiety-Fishing?

George Bernard Shaw once said that *"People become attached to their burdens sometimes more than the burdens are attached to them."*

That is still true. Anxiety had become so much a way of life for me that I used to feel precarious if I experienced a glimpse of life *without* any particular worries, whether for a few seconds or a couple of hours. My sister once rightly told me, "You're not happy unless you are anxious about something."

It is easy to start 'fishing' for things to worry about without realizing it. Perversely, anxiety can be my safe place, just because it has become the default position.

If there are no particular worries intruding at present, don't fish! Enjoy the moment. This is an opportunity to have a break from anxiety, which is very well-deserved!

Worry Beliefs

Why do I fish for anxieties? Why is anxiety my familiar default position and why, as my sister said, am I not happy unless I am anxious about something?

I fish because of what are called 'worry-beliefs'.

Many things fuel anxiety, but a main driver of our anxiety is our worry-beliefs.

It is important to understand that these are *not* the same as individual worries.

Instead, worry-beliefs are convictions we have that make us believe our anxiety is necessary.

When I was introduced to the concept of worry-beliefs, it seemed to make no sense. I even felt very indignant about it: "What?!! Of course I don't believe my anxiety is necessary – it's a curse! I've spent my whole life trying to control it!"

I realized in therapy, however, that I do indeed believe my anxiety (or rather, over-anxiety) is necessary, however much of a curse it is, because of my worry-beliefs.

Understanding the concept of worry-beliefs proved very helpful for me.

For example, one of my worry-beliefs is: "If I worry about a person, no harm will come to them." This fuels my anxieties about individual people. For example: "If my partner is travelling, I need to be worrying about him, because my worrying will make sure he will travel safely."

To help clarify further what I mean, I set out three of my own worry-beliefs in the text that follows, including further explanation of the one that I have just mentioned.

Under each one you'll see that I list the behaviours that that particular one might have led to, followed by the thoughts I used to challenge that particular worry-belief.

Challenging them in this way helps to reduce the fuel for my individual anxieties.

Everybody will have their own particular set of worry-beliefs, although many people will have very similar ones.

Three of My Particular Worry-Beliefs

WORRY-BELIEF 1

"If I worry about a person, no harm will come to them." Here, my worry is a sort of 'insurance policy' to ensure the safety of my loved ones.

RESULTING BEHAVIOURS
- Ringing the person unnecessarily to reassure myself that he/she is OK
- Asking other people for reassurance
- Performing rituals, such as those outlined in Chapter Three

HOW I CHALLENGED THIS

Worry-Belief 1 is based on a superstitious way of thinking. As I have described in Chapter Three, superstition sits deep within the human psyche. Beliefs based on superstition can therefore be very powerful, and dismissing anxious thoughts by saying, "You're just being superstitious" is not helpful.

Instead, I try and resist using worry as a sort of 'insurance policy' to ensure the safety of my loved ones. To help me manage these Worry-Belief 1 behaviours, I visualize two unrelated objects, such as an apple and a bicycle, and note how one does not influence the other in any way. This reminds me that if I am worrying about a person, my fears do not influence what happens to them.

WORRY-BELIEF 2

"I deserve to be anxious. I don't deserve for life to be easy".

RESULTING BEHAVIOUR

General anxiety behaviours, such as ritualization or repetitive checking.

HOW I CHALLENGED THIS

Life is not easy for many people, but the key word in this worry-belief is 'deserve'. The conviction that I don't *deserve* for life to be easy is one with no obvious cause. I hold the view that this belief originates largely from lack of self-confidence, which I believe to be one of the root causes of GAD.

Although I have never known why I lacked self-confidence, I knew that building up self-confidence would help reduce my anxiety and OCD, and this has proved to be true.

Building up confidence can take a long time, but in the meantime I remind myself that I deserve at least as much happiness in life as the next person.

WORRY-BELIEF 3

"Anxiety has been there all my life. I didn't ask for it and I don't have a choice about it."

RESULTING BEHAVIOURS
Any or all anxiety behaviours.

HOW I CHALLENGED THIS

It might be true that I have always had anxiety and didn't ask for it. But it isn't true that I don't have a choice about living with it. Actually, I've seen that I *do* have a choice . . .

Breaking down my worry beliefs goes a long way towards taking the power out of the worries themselves.

Worry Belief Walls

In reality, my individual worry-beliefs and their consequent behaviours, and individual anxieties and worries, merge and overlap. I do not spend time thinking which individual worry is caused by which worry-belief; anxiety does not work as neatly as that.

However, matching my anxiety behaviours to my worry-beliefs, as far as I can, helps me to manage GAD in general.

After I first had therapy, I came to realize that I had much more control over my anxiety and OCD than I thought I did, albeit by practising difficult strategies. Control lies in repeatedly bringing myself back to managing my anxiety behaviours, the crux of which is described in 'Breaking the Anxiety Cycle' in Chapter Two, which is also the mainstay of Cognitive Behavioural Therapy (CBT).

Life Toolkit strategies from this chapter:

48. If there are no particular worries intruding at present, don't fish! Enjoy the moment. This is an opportunity to have a break from anxiety, which is very well-deserved!
49. Try to resist using worry as a sort of 'insurance policy' to ensure the safety of loved ones. To help manage this Worry-Belief behaviour, visualize two unrelated objects, such as an apple and a bicycle, and note how one does not influence the other in any way.
50. Building up confidence can take a long time, but in the meantime remind yourself that you deserve at least as much happiness in life as the next person.
51. It might be true that you have always had anxiety and didn't ask for it. But it isn't true that you don't have a choice about living with it. Actually, try and see that you *do* have a choice.
52. Breaking down my worry beliefs goes a long way towards taking the power out of the worries themselves.
53. Matching your anxiety behaviours to your worry-beliefs, as far as you can, can help you to manage GAD in general.

CHAPTER 13

INTOLERANCE OF UNCERTAINTY (IOU)

How Can Uncertainty be Managed Effectively?

A big driver of anxiety is what is known as Intolerance of Uncertainty (IOU).

For me, this has been the crux of my anxiety, and it used to affect me in two main ways:

1. I mentally over-planned for some terribly imaginary scenario, in the misplaced belief that I would be more prepared if the scenario became a reality.
2. I continually had to resist the urge to check unnecessarily that everything was alright.

In short, I tried very hard to control the uncertain nature of life.

BUT... life *is* uncertain, as everybody knows.

So how come I have so much difficulty dealing with this notion when many others take it in their stride?

I don't know – but what I do know is that it was important to learn how I could effectively *manage* those feelings of uncertainty.

Life with intolerance of uncertainty feels precarious, like walking a route filled with terrifying obstacles, whereas life with an acceptance of uncertainty feels much more controllable.

I have learnt a range of useful strategies for dealing with this Intolerance of Uncertainty:

I pretend that I am tolerant of uncertainty

and try to behave/act as far as possible as if uncertainty doesn't unduly bother me. I have found this breaks into the behaviour block of the GAD cycle and, over time, has helped me to mitigate the intolerance.

I think "Alpha'!

I'm a confident, self-assured Alpha Person!" Uncertainty, intolerance and anxiety are 'Delta' behaviours. (See Chapter Sixteen for further explanation of this).

I turn negative mental images into positive ones.

For example, if I am out and my son has friends round to our home, rather than fearing them having accidents or inadvertently setting the home on fire, I imagine them enjoying their evening together. I make a conscious effort to prevent myself slipping into imagining the worst-case scenario.

I keep everyday life as organized as possible

so as not to have any unnecessary uncertainty. This removes avoidable uncertainties, such as running late. ('A little bit of OCD can be a good thing'.)

I deal with small uncertainties first.

For example, I might or might not be able to go for a walk with my friend later. It will depend on whether she will have finished her work in time.

I consider uncertainty in terms of percentages of certainty;

the situation might have a higher percentage of certainty than I initially think it does.

I look for the positives in the uncertainty of life.

For example, I might win the lottery or find a great opportunity in an unexpected situation.

I keep my physical environment reasonably ordered

so that I can minimize uncertainty at home by avoiding things like misplacing items.

The Power of Creativity

In Chapter One I mentioned that I believe an active imagination can be partly responsible for excessive anxiety. And it definitely holds true for me that when I'm creative I feel a lot less anxious.

My cartoons, which I love doing, are my main creative outlet; I find creating them very anxiety-reducing.

I have also found it hugely helpful to do something craft or DIY-based when I feel anxious. It offers a great distraction and can also be very therapeutic; it is as if my worries are diverted into the tangible piece of work.

Life Toolkit strategies from this chapter:

54. Life with unmanaged feelings of uncertainty feels precarious, whereas life with an acceptance of uncertainty feels much more controllable.
55. Pretend that you are tolerant of uncertainty.
56. Think "Alpha'!
57. Turn negative mental images into positive ones.
58. Keep everyday life as organized as possible.
59. Deal with *small* uncertainties first.
60. Consider uncertainty in terms of percentages of certainty.
61. Look for the positives in the uncertainty of life.
62. Keep your physical environment reasonably ordered.
63. It can be helpful to do something craft or DIY-based when you feel anxious.

CHAPTER 14

IT'S NOT ALL ABOUT ME

Don't let anxiety make life harder for myself and others.

Behaving as if multiple disasters are lying in wait for me all the time meant I was carrying too much and wearing myself out.

It also meant that I could come across as difficult, needy and demanding of others at times.

My good friends accept my idiosyncrasies, and were patient with me. Even so, I had to consider them too, and accept that they might not have the same burdensome view of things as I did.

My Loved Ones are not Therapists!

Friends and loved ones give crucial support when I am dealing with fear and anxiety – but it's important to remember they are not superhuman, and they have issues and anxieties of their own.

In a desperate morass of dark fear, it can be instinctive to grab repeatedly at apparent lifelines offered by friends. But in order to prevent myself becoming overly dependent on friends' reassurance, and becoming an 'anxiety bore', I try really hard not to do this every time.

My loved ones will support me but they are not therapists!

How Family and Friends Can Help

Family and friends will often try to help in ways that, unbeknown to them, actually do *not* help in the long term, such as through offering reassurance.

For example, if a friend says, "Don't worry, I'm sure it will be fine," it generally doesn't help, as it gives no support in helping me to *stop* my anxious behaviours .

If a friend, on the other hand, were to say something like: "Shall we work through to the actual nub of your worry?" this would be useful.

If I ask, "Did I really switch off the iron?" it is comforting, of course, to be reassured by a loved one that I *have*, but it does not help me to escape from that type of worry the next time.

When I have explained to those close to me what helps and what doesn't, and how they can support me constructively, their help can make an incalculable difference.

It is often a big relief just to share with others when I am having difficulty with something, as then I don't have the added stress of trying to 'act normal' when I am struggling on the inside.

So if I need help, I don't disguise it. I'm upfront about it.

For instance, my way of telling my partner these days that I want to talk about a worry is to say, "I'm on a worry mountain," or to describe the worry and say, "Should I be worried about this?"

This way, I make it clear that I need help with an anxiety problem, and, together, we can talk through the strategies that might help.

I used to interact with others in a more round-about way – trying to get people to help me without actually telling them I was struggling.

Below is an example of a worrying situation in a social context, and a choice of ways to react to it.

Suppose I have a worry that any food I do not prepare myself is contaminated – and a friend asks me to a meal at a restaurant.

I have a number of simple choices:

A. Disguising Anxiety
B. Denying Anxiety
C. Externalizing Anxiety

A. Disguising Anxiety: I can try to get the friend to reassure me about the food, whilst keeping my anxiety secret. So, I could make something up, such as, "I had a friend who got really bad food poisoning after eating in a restaurant." To which I hope the friend would say something like, "Oh everything is fine at *this* restaurant, I've eaten here several times."

This is a way of manipulating another person to say something to alleviate my anxiety, although the manipulation might not be completely deliberate.

Like the scenario of trying to lead someone into a different course of action that I described in my Underground journey tale in Chapter Six, I am making up scenarios to disguise my worrying thoughts. I am seeking reassurance and trying to disguise this fact.

B. Denying Anxiety: I can deny the worry by keeping it to myself and trying to manage it with various strategies.

This means dealing with the worry alone, whilst trying to be sociable with someone else, so I will have the extra pressure of trying to act naturally whilst working hard on the anxiety and feeling distressed. It is very difficult not to seem distant and preoccupied in such a situation.

C. Externalizing Anxiety: I can say to the person, "I have anxieties about food when I haven't prepared it myself. I'd like to eat with you but I'm not sure if I can eat there." If the person is one of my trusted friends, they are likely to want to help me.

They might make a joke about it: "Oh yes, you're going to be *really* ill after eating there!" which might help to lighten the mood and diffuse my anxiety.

They might refuse to accommodate my anxiety and say, "I'm going to eat there anyway. Feel free to just have a drink." Again, this might give me a different perspective on the worry.

Or they might do something else entirely – I can't know. The main point, however, is that I would no longer be alone with the anxiety and no longer have to hide it.

Out of the three options, Behaviour C (Externalizing Anxiety) is the best response, as by being honest with the friend, I allow them to try to help me.

Someone who knows me well is likely to be initially bemused and eventually irritated if I use Behaviour **A** (Disguising Anxiety) with them. They will sense the disguise and pretence, and might even feel I am trying to hoodwink them.

However if I use Behaviour **C** (Externalising Anxiety) the friend can support me.

Years ago, I commonly used Behaviour **A** (Disguising Anxiety) as I believed that admitting anxiety would make me appear weak. I felt I would never be able to come across as an independent, self-sufficient person if I admitted all my worries, even though

I knew that underneath my anxiety problem I *was* independent and self-sufficient.

It may seem strange now but, early on, I didn't realize that my level of anxiety was 'abnormal'. And I therefore didn't recognize it as a problem that could be treated.

To draw a comparison, when I was 15, I started wearing glasses. Before the glasses, I hadn't realized that my sight was not 20:20; I had just assumed that everybody else's sight was similar to mine. But as soon as I got the glasses, the world became so much more wonderfully clear.

In the same way, although I was very stressed by fear and anxiety, I was in my twenties before I realized I had an anxiety condition that I could actually get help with.

Before that, I had only been aware that everyone else seemed to cope with life generally much better than I did.

Given that this made me feel inferior and embarrassed, I used disguising behaviour to try to get reassurance and alleviate the anxiety. But as I have emphasized in Chapter Nine, reassurance-seeking for OCD and GAD worries only tends to make the problems worse in the end – trapping us in a vicious circle.

Below is an example of the healthier Behaviour **C** (Externalizing Anxiety) in action in real life:

I have a friend who is frequently anxious about whether food is safe to eat.

Sometimes she is worried that, although a food item is within its sell-by date, it has not been constantly in the fridge, and sometimes she is anxious about whether something has been cooked properly.

This kind of worry can, at times, of course, be completely legitimate. However, the friend in question frequently worries unnecessarily with regard to food.

She is aware that she has OCD tendencies and that she has no real need to worry. But, as is common with anxiety, she can quickly start catastrophizing.

Sometimes she will ring me when she has this difficulty with food items, and will start the conversation by saying, "I've got a 'food' question".

This is very honest and straightforward; she has externalized her anxieties and shared them with me.

I therefore know immediately why she has rung me and feel engaged to help in any way I can.

Suppose, instead of doing this, the friend rang me on some pretext, then steered the conversation in a certain way so that she could drop in a question near the end about the particular food fear in the hope that I would reassure her.

This means that instead of saying something like, "Can I check this chicken with you?", she might say, "Mmm, speaking of dinner, I've got this chicken here. You have to be careful with chicken. I wonder if it's alright?" etc.

This kind of disguising behaviour would risk irritating me, to be honest, as I would probably sense, as someone who knows her well, the *real* reason for her call and wish she would just come out and confront it.

Using Friends to Help you Know if a Worry is Normal

A worry that sometimes bothers me when I have gone out is that I might have left my hairdryer on.

Leaving a hairdryer or other device on, and therefore inadvertently causing a risk of fire, is a common type of anxiety for me (and, I am sure, for countless others affected by anxiety).

I know that a modern hairdryer will cut out if it overheats.

I might know deep down that I switched it off.

I might recall that I didn't hear it running when I left home, and so on.

But, as I have mentioned, rational thoughts like this do not necessarily help lessen intrusive thoughts.

All I can think about is the miniscule chance that I left the hairdryer on and the even more miniscule chance that this will cause a fire.

I am 99.999% sure that no harm will be done, but I feel that the results of my leaving the hairdryer on would be so devastating that I need to worry about the remaining 0.001%.

I imagine the sights, smells and noises of the fire in all their terrible detail.

In the midst of all this anxiety, it can be difficult to tell whether the main intrusive thought is a 'normal' one (ie one that anyone else would be bothered by) or a GAD/OCD-related one.

This is where I need my partner, or another trusted loved one, to help me by using honesty, humour and some of the actions in the list of examples that follows:

1. Stop me from checking things so obsessively, for example, that I have checked the front door is locked, more than eight times when I leave the house. This number can then be reduced the next time, and so on.
2. Use humour to counter reassurance-seeking—to help give me a different perspective and direct me away from my anxious delusions.
3. Distract me by talking to me about something else that will engage me.
4. Block access to letting me wash cups (or whatever other object I may be obsessing on) more than, say, five times that day (due to contamination fear).
5. If possible, remove items that would enable my checking and self-reassurance behaviours (eg washing-up liquid).

These days I no longer need the last two behavioural supports, but the first three still play their part in my life occasionally.

Life Toolkit strategies from this chapter:

64. It can be instinctive to grab repeatedly at apparent lifelines offered by friends. But in order to prevent yourself becoming overly dependent on friends' reassurance, and becoming an 'anxiety bore', try hard not to do this every time.
65. When you have explained to those close to you what helps and what doesn't, and how they can support you constructively, their help can make an incalculable difference.
66. Out of the three options, Externalizing Anxiety (C) is the best response, as by being honest with the friend, you will allow them to try to help you.

CHAPTER 15

WHAT'S NORMAL?

What's a Normal Level of Anxiety?

I have learnt that it is crucial to recognize when my anxiety is moving from a 'normal' level to an excessive level.

Let me give another car-driving example.

For many people, there is some natural anxiety involved in driving on motorways. This is necessary because it is what keeps us alert and driving safely. **That's OK.**

I used to drive on the motorway quite a lot before a gap of about 12 years when I didn't have a car. Then, when I got a car again, I had a couple of lessons to help me get used to being back at the wheel. Yet when I went back to driving on the motorway again, I wasn't as confident as more experienced drivers, and I felt anxious. **That's OK.**

I am not bothered by having a different level of worry to the next person if there is a good reason for it, as in this situation. I accept this kind of worry as perfectly normal behaviour. **That's OK.**

If, however, I had decided I was too anxious to drive on the motorway ever again, and taken no steps about this, it would have meant I was giving in to my anxiety. It would have meant that I was allowing my anxiety to dictate what I am able or not able to do in life. **That's NOT OK.**

So I took steps, and had a couple of motorway-driving refresher lessons, and now I'm fine.

Tolerance-Level Anxiety

As I am prone to GAD, I have to accept that I will always have a certain (above normal) level of anxiety. I should neither deny this by pretending it isn't there nor give in to it, because either of these behaviours will just make my anxiety worse.

My aim is to keep anxiety at a tolerable level – a level that I can manage.

Some anxiety is, for example, necessary for optimal performance in certain circumstances, like just before a job interview. And it will then disappear. This is perfectly normal.

However, if I expect *all* anxiety to be eliminated on a worry-by-worry basis by, for example, reassurance-seeking, then I'm likely to go through life on somewhat of an anxiety rollercoaster – constantly experiencing low-level troughs, followed by inevitable recurring peaks. And this peak-trough-peak pattern of anxieties is unpredictable, exhausting and impossible to control.

If, however, I continue to practise the Toolkit strategies in this book, I can manage my anxiety effectively and my life need not be an all-consuming fight with it, which is great!

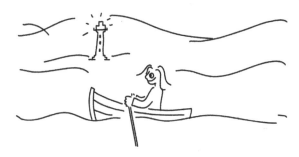

There will always be ups and downs of some sort. A major life event can trigger or exacerbate anxiety, and sometimes anxiety can increase for no apparent reason. This is the case for everybody.

I need to keep alert and keep my GAD management strategies ever to-hand so that when it starts to rise, I am on the case.

Life Toolkit strategies from this chapter:

67. It is crucial to recognize when your anxiety is moving from a 'normal' level to an excessive level.
68. You may have to accept that you will always have a certain (above normal) level of anxiety. You should neither deny this by pretending it isn't there nor give in to it, because this just makes it worse.
69. Your aim is to keep anxiety at a tolerable level – a level that you can manage.

CHAPTER 16

ALPHA AND DELTA BEHAVIOURS

There are many ways to categorize and label human behaviours, for example 'extrovert'/'introvert', 'relaxed'/'stressy'. Personally, I have found that the descriptions 'Alpha' and 'Delta' are very helpful.

Distinguishing between these two has been crucial for me – both in life generally, and, in particular, with regard to my anxiety disorders.

I will explain these terms in a moment but it's worth firstly knowing that, although a Delta person might be Alpha about certain things and at certain times, and vice versa, a person *generally* displays either Alpha or Delta qualities.

Alpha and Delta: Recognize Yourself?

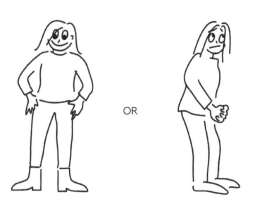

OR

Twelve Typical ALPHA Qualities

1. Confident
2. Independent
3. Self-possessed
4. Assertive
5. Decisive
6. With courage of convictions
7. Physically open and upright
8. Stylish
9. Calm
10. Self-assured
11. Driven
12. Forward-looking

Twelve Typical DELTA Qualities

1. Unconfident
2. Subservient
3. Flustered
4. Apologetic
5. Lacking conviction
6. Feeling doubtful, or guilty
7. Physically cowed
8. Down-dressing
9. Anxious
10. Seeking approval
11. Passive
12. Tendency to look back (in time)

'Act Alpha'

I explained earlier (in Chapters One and Twelve) that I believe lack of confidence to have been one of the underlying causes of my GAD.

As you can see from the lists above, the behaviours and feelings that go with lack of confidence tend to be Delta ones.

I have realized, when tackling GAD, to aim to be as Alpha as possible by *showing* Alpha behaviours even when I don't feel them!

Obviously one cannot change the habits of a lifetime overnight. But 'acting Alpha' helped me over time actually to *be* more Alpha, and consequently more confident.

Some behaviours can be changed from Delta to Alpha quite quickly and easily. For example, walking tall, or dressing a bit differently if down-dress is usually the norm.

Long before I became aware of the Alpha/Delta concept, I asked a colleague who was always very stylish if she would go shopping with me. This was a hugely positive experience. She guided me to choose clothes that gave me an air of confidence and poise. Although I didn't know it at the time, this was my first entry into the world of Alpha. We also bonded through the process and have been close friends ever since.

Life Toolkit strategy from this chapter:

70. It is helpful, when tackling GAD, to aim to be as Alpha as possible by *showing* Alpha behaviours even when you don't feel them!

CHAPTER 17

KEEPING ON THE CASE

Keeping on Top of Anxiety Management

During the time that I had to concentrate very hard on reduction techniques, it was sometimes tempting to 'give myself a break' from managing my anxiety.

For example, I might have been doing well with starting to reduce my over-checking habits. Then, one day, when, perhaps I was not feeling well or I had something on my mind connected with work, it could be all too easy to think, "I've got enough on my plate as it is today. I'm going to give in to over-checking this once, because I can't deal with the stress of checking-reduction today on top of everything else."

This is really understandable because anxiety management requires effort and tenacity, and on bad days I might simply feel that I didn't have the mental resources for it.

In the past I have 'skipped' my efforts for a day or two because there was just too much else going on in life.

Try not to skip reduction techniques on bad days.

The key here, however, is not let giving in to such thoughts become a habit. So when I *could* get myself to persevere with my reduction strategies even on such bad days, it was really worth making the effort to do so.

However, if I *did* 'skip' on occasions, I tried not to give yourself a hard time about it. I simply worked my techniques back up again, which was quicker than working them up for the first time. And the crucial thing was not to let a one-day skip drag on into several days or a week of skipping.

People who take medications for long-term conditions can sometimes think after a while, "It's fine, I don't need these pills now as I'm doing well" and stop taking them. But the associated health problems can then return, because in fact it had been the medication that was keeping them functioning well.

My anxiety management techniques are like a form of medication. It is tempting to think, "I don't need to do this anymore, as I'm fine now." But then, before I know it, the anxiety can creep up on me, flooring me when I'm least expecting it.

So I know that it's of utmost importance to keep on top of my anxiety management techniques.

It is best never to let the hard-won techniques in my toolkit 'gather dust'. Instead, I must always keep them honed and mentally within reach for when I need them.

Anxiety Management is a DIY Process

This book has continually emphasized how important it is for treatment for anxiety to be self-driven . . .

Although there is a lot of external help available for managing anxiety conditions, ultimately my management of GAD and anxiety has been about *me* taking control.

And this is my message to *you*, the reader of this little book. Therapists can teach management strategies, be supportive and guide you if you are going off course, but it is YOU who has to do the work; the vast majority of treatment for OCD and GAD is done outside the therapy sessions. This can feel like an initially daunting prospect, but those close to you can support you as you go, steadily, one step at a time.

Help is Available

If you need more support, remember that help is out there, so there's no need to suffer in silence!

Just reach out – whether to your local doctor, health centre or any other medical or mental health professional.

Seeking professional help is what allowed me to first learn how to manage my OCD and GAD. I had an initial course of Cognitive Behavioural Therapy (CBT) many years ago, and since then have done three 'refresher' courses during particularly difficult periods, usually after life-changing events.

So, although OCD and GAD can make you feel very lonely at times, remember that you are not alone!

I hope you have found the anxiety-related insights, tales and strategies that I have shared in these pages useful.

I really believe that they will help you to sweep away that Anxiety Spider – and to keep out of the dreaded Anxiety Web – so that you can live a positive and fulfilled life.

Life Toolkit strategies from this chapter:

71. Try not to skip your reduction techniques on bad days.
72. It is best never to let the hard-won techniques in your toolkit 'gather dust'. Keep them honed and mentally within reach for when you need them.
73. This book has continually emphasised how important it is for treatment for anxiety to be self-driven.
74. Although there is a lot of external help available for managing anxiety conditions, ultimately it is about YOU taking control.
75. If you need more support, remember that help is out there, so there's no need to suffer in silence!

Wishing you every success with your anxiety management!

ABOUT CHERISH EDITIONS

Cherish Editions is a bespoke self-publishing service for authors of mental health, wellbeing and inspirational books. As a division of Trigger Publishing, the UK's leading independent mental health and wellbeing publisher, we are experienced in creating and selling positive, responsible, important and inspirational books, which work to de-stigmatise the issues around mental health and improve the mental health and wellbeing of those who read our titles.

Founded by Adam Shaw, a mental health advocate, author and philanthropist, and leading psychologist Lauren Callaghan, Cherish Editions aims to publish books that provide advice, support and inspiration. We nurture our authors so that their stories can unfurl on the page, helping them to share their uplifting and moving stories.

Cherish Editions is unique in that a percentage of the profits from the sale of our books goes directly to leading mental health charity Shawmind, to deliver its vision to provide support for those experiencing mental ill health.

Find out more about Cherish Editions by visiting cherisheditions.com or by joining us on:
Twitter @cherisheditions
Facebook @cherisheditions
Instagram @cherisheditions

Cherish
EDITIONS

ABOUT SHAW MIND

A proportion of profits from the sale of all Cherish books go to their sister charity, Shawmind, also founded by Adam Shaw and Lauren Callaghan. The charity aims to ensure that everyone has access to mental health resources whenever they need them.

You can find out more about the work Shaw Mind do by visiting their website: shawmind.org or joining them on

Twitter @Shaw_Mind
Facebook @shawmindUK
Instagram @Shaw_Mind

Your Local Mental Health & Wellbeing Charity

ABOUT THE AUTHOR

Helena was an art consultant before working in part-time business roles while bringing up her son. She has degrees in History of Art/English, and Graphic Design. She has practised CBT techniques for thirty years as a patient, initially attending a 1:1 course in Isaac Marks' department at the Institute of Psychiatry. She has since updated her techniques via three local courses. She manages GAD and OCD herself, very successfully.

Her cartoons have appeared in workshops for the NHS and the Business Psychology Company, and in company magazines. They appear regularly in the weekly bellringing magazine, *The Ringing World*. Most recently, she has finished illustrating a children's book *Nicolas and the Six Bells* by David Ackerman, published by Gabriel Books.

You can find out more by visiting her website: www.HelenaCartoonist.com